CONVIDA MULTIMEDIA

The internet is a vast treasure-trove of information.
Cultural riches abound there, waiting to be discovered.
Anyone can explore it easily with a bit of surfing and some simple mouse clicks.

But it's just as easy to get lost in the labyrinth of available information!
What if an expert did the footwork for you?
In these books dedicated experts spin a common thread.

That's what our multi-media books do:
A topic - a common thread - an entertaining script - and a hundred or more lively examples from the internet.
It's the modern-day concept of the 'traditional' book with interactive content. The multi-media book.

Intercultural Book-Series

Cultural Heritage of Humanity

Discover – Admire – Understand

Volume 4

**Multimedia compositions
for reading with all the senses.
The BOOKS with CLICKS**

e² books – auvideo books – print editions

**CONVIDA
Gesellschaft zur Förderung der kulturellen Begegnung und des Tourismus mbH & Co KG
www.multi-media-books.com**

THE VOICE

Annette Betanski

Combined print, ebook and audio edition
Audio-version read by the author

This little book is meant to inspire curiosity and wonder about the human voice. It is certainly meant to shed some light on various aspects of singing, but mainly it is a guided tour meant to cultivate even more appreciation of the magnificent phenomenon of singing and the human voice.
The author Annette Betanski attended the Royal Conservatory of Music in Toronto for Vocal Performance and then completed an Artist Diploma at McGill University in Montreal. Since graduating, she has been a singer mainly in the area of classical music, chamber music and opera, and has been a singing teacher for the last 18 years in Boston and now in Berlin.
You can find out more about the author by visiting her website:
http://annettebetanski.com/de

© All contents published in these works are subject to German and international copyright and neighbouring right laws. Any use that is prohibited by these laws requires the prior written permission of the author or the respective right holder. A Click (e²Book) will lead to important **Technical and Legal Information** at the end of the book.

Die Deutsche Nationalbibliothek verzeichnet diese Publikation in der Deutschen Nationalbibliographie, detaillierte Daten sind im Internet über http://dnb.dnb.de abrufbar.
The Deutsche Nationalbibliothek has listed this publication in Deutsche Nationalbibliographie, detailed data are accessable on the Internet under http://dnb.dnb.de .

© 2017 Annette Betanski
Cover/Einbandentwurf© Hauptstadtpixel Birgit Fuhrmann
Foto für Einband/cover© fotolia akamaraqu@fotolia.com Abstract colorful watercolor background for graphic design
3 Fotos farbig/coloured Seite/page 3
© fotolia masterzphotofo, yurf15 und Sergey Nivens
© 2017 Publisher Convida Gesellschaft zur Förderung der kulturellen Begegnung und des Tourismus mbH & Co KG
Herstellung:
BoD – Books on Demand, Norderstedt
ISBN 978-3-946434-04-7

Table of Contents

With a Click (e^2Book) you will get to the required subject.

The Thrill of Multimedia

All of our books

are available as eBooks and also in print format.

In both cases, the audiobook version may be included with no extra charge.

Reading online you reach the linked objects by direct *CLICK.*

For off-line reading, you need access to internet content via

LinkLists.

Open the multimedia links step by step whilst reading.

Or open the

PlayList

(first LinkList position) for streaming the "Auvideo"-version.
To get the respective LinkList :

- Go to our Website www.multi-media-books.com
- Click "LinkLists" in the menu
- Insert the document-number of the book segment you want to study (see text of the book)
- Click and Click and Click...

When you see a speech bubble, it alerts you to the fact that there is a link associated with the text. That means it's time to *CLICK*! In the audio-version you only have to watch for the announcement of a *CLICK* in case of a text link. Then you may stop streaming and switch over to the text- object (see LinkList - positions). All the other objects appear automatically (streaming).

video link

text link

If you are streaming and one of the links has been removed (thereby stopping the streaming), or if you would like to skip certain videos, **simply click on the Youtube icon at the bottom righthand corner. The Playlist will appear on the screen, and you can skip to the next video.**

Optimal impressions of the audio-version you will get on your TV. Ask an Expert how to manage it on your specific model.

01 The Amazing Human Voice

Doc-Number/ LinkList 1: *34718-4711*

The human voice is an extraordinary thing. Expression through our vocalizations is as primordial as we are as a species. Throughout human history and throughout all cultures and civilizations the human voice has been ours to communicate with - to express emotions, thoughts, ideas, stories and our human spirit. The voice is the original human instrument, the instrument we all possess, whether we 'play it' or not. And arguably, the instrument that speaks most directly to us, heart to heart, soul to soul. It is the instrument which is made of living flesh and bone and the air we breathe. Whether it's an individual singing, or whether it's a group of voices joined together, this fascinating and mysterious instrument never ceases to capture our attention, our imagination and awe.

02 Who can benefit from this book?

Anybody with a keen interest in singing and all things 'voice' can benefit from this book. Singers, aspiring singers and passionate fans of the voice will get to dive a little deeper in their understanding of how this amazing instrument works. No one, particular vocal technique is being put forward, rather, it is an exploration of the phenomenon of voice and singing in general. It's a great supplement to university freshmen in their vocal studies and a perfect companion for anybody who is beginning to explore their own voice. Simply put, it's for anyone who loves the human voice and wants to know more about it. Who knows, maybe a budding young voice scientist is among you, or a soon-to-be overtone singer, beatboxer, voice impressionist, opera diva or rock star!

03 What this book is, and what it isn't.

We'll survey different topics and look at various vocal traditions from opera to pop, overtone singing to beat-boxing and many others in between. Again, this is *not* a book which promotes any one, particular vocal technique or ideology, it is *not* a how-to guide or instruction manual, although there are some sections on various vocal theories and techniques. This little book is meant to inspire curiosity and wonder about the human voice. It is certainly meant to shed some light on various aspects of singing, but mainly it is a guided tour meant to cultivate even more appreciation of the magnificent phenomenon of singing and the human voice. It is a collection of internet links, which I have selected and organized. I might add a brief explanation, comment, personal opinion or observation about what I present, but I leave a good portion of the information to be transmitted by the links themselves. Remember that for every subject briefly touched upon, there exists the possibility to go much deeper. For every subject, some specialist, singer, musicologist or other professional has devoted their life to its in-depth study. So consider this an inspired interaction with an informed friend who shares your interest in the human voice. Many varied topics will be touched upon.

Consider it a 'tasting menu' at a favorite restaurant.
Feel free to try everything, or skip over the dishes you're already familiar with or don't grab your fancy.

There are not only performance and singing links, but many information links as well. The book is designed so that you can skip around, however, if you find you are missing some information pertaining to the link you're viewing, you may have to backtrack.

Some links are more academic and some are more performance-oriented. I do recommend you click on the initial links that explain how the human voice functions as this will significantly deepen your appreciation of topics to come.

04 A brief word about your author.

I have been naturally fascinated by singing since childhood. On my kindergarten report card my teacher stated, "Annette still has trouble buttoning up her coat... but shows a marked interest in singing." At the age of 9, I joined the Canadian Children's Opera Chorus and had the opportunity to be on opera and concert hall stages as a choir member and as a young soloist until the age of 14. Then, as a teenager, I sang in rock band. We rehearsed in the basement of our drummer's mom's suburban home and even won a 'Battle of the Bands' at a local Ramada Hotel. As entertaining as it was, I soon realized that my fascination with vocal sound product ion went beyond what I was experiencing. I found myself trying to mimic opera singers and produce the same incredible sounds they did. Pretty soon, my formal voice studies began. I attended the Royal Conservatory of Music in Toronto for Vocal Performance and then completed an Artist Diploma at McGill

University in Montreal. Since graduating, I have been a singer mainly in the area of classical music, chamber music and opera, and I have been a singing teacher for the last 18 years in Boston and now in Berlin. Guiding and assisting others to grow and discover the natural wonders of their own voice seems to have been my calling. Over the years I have never stopped learning and exploring this grand subject through work with many other professionals in the field. I'm happy to report that I have mastered buttoning up my own coat, but my marked interest in singing hasn't left me.

05 Discovering the Voice

Because much of the human voice is internal and invisible to the naked eye, its workings seem mysterious. Some singers have attained such command over their voices that it's hard to imagine that generally speaking, we all possess the very same anatomy. Some singers themselves have little idea of how they manipulate their bodies in order to produce certain sounds. Some operate from an instinctive or culturally taught vocal tradition, without knowing what actually is occurring in their bodies while singing. Others, upon extensive study, enquiry, practice, and with the advancement of science have learned much about and even peered into the 'invisible workings' of the human voice thereby uncovering some of its mysteries. (Here I would add that, personally, I don't judge 'trained voices' as necessarily superior to 'untrained' voices.)

Before we get into some of the exciting and diverse topics to come, let's lay down a basic foundation of understanding of the human vocal instrument. Every subject to come will hold significantly greater depth when you can basically understand

and visualize how the voice works.

06 How the Voice Works

Let's dive into those 'invisible workings' of the voice. For those of you who haven't seen or imagined your *vocal cords* (also known as *vocal folds*), seeing them for the first time may be a revelation. In the following 2 clips we'll see inside a young woman's healthy *larynx,* which is commonly known as the '*voice box*'. The larynx is the organ which houses the vocal cords. To find your own larynx, place your fingers on your throat and feel for a skeletal-like structure beneath. You will most likely find a central ridge and elevation which is commonly known as the '*Adam's Apple*' and is generally more pronounced in men than in women. (This is the angle of the thyroid cartilage that surrounds the larynx.) If you hum you will feel a vibration there. This is the result of your vocal folds vibrating together a couple of hundred times per second – just in a simple hum!

We'll look inside the workings of the larynx with the help of a machine called a stroboscope, which is an instrument that is used to make a cyclically moving object appear to be slow-moving. In essence, it's a slow-motion camera. This is necessary because the vocal cords oscillate (vibrate together) at a rate of anywhere from 100 to 1000 times per second, depending on the pitch of the sound we're making. This is obviously beyond the ability of the naked eye to perceive. To really see the vocal folds and how they move we need to significantly slow things down.

In the following 2 clips we will be looking directly at the vocal folds from above. Even though the subjects are female, if you happen to be a man your anatomy here looks essentially the same although your vocal folds (the 2 whitish strands which vibrate together) may be thicker. Pay attention to what is happening as the subject is asked to sing higher and lower pitches, and also what happens when she is just simply breathing and not making sound. Notice when the vocal folds are coming together, moving apart and when they are stretching. Are they getting longer, shorter or remaining the same?

As you watch the vocal folds vibrating, you may notice some little bumps and sticky bits on the vocal folds. In this case, it is just a little normal mucous. Ideally, the mucous should be thin and there to provide necessary and smooth lubrication. You will see two fleshy bumps at the top and to either side of the vocal folds, these are cartilage that make up part of the structure of the larynx. Also, you may notice a flap-like structure moving into the screen from below which resembles a lip. This is called the *epiglottis* which is a flap made of elastic cartilage which folds to prevent food from going down into 'the wrong hole': that is, it directs food into the *esophagus* (*the 'food pipe'*) and closes off and protects the *trachea* (*the 'wind pipe'*) when eating/swallowing.

20 Stroboscopy of Vocal Cords

10 normal female Vocal Cords

OK, ready to take a look inside?

0010/THEORY 0020/THEORY

Yes! That's more or less what you look like inside your own throat too!

Did you observe the movement of the vocal folds? Did you see how it was necessary for the two sides to come together (to close) in order for the sound to be produced? Maybe you also noticed that when she sang a higher pitch the vocal folds got longer and thinner. When she lowered the pitch the cords got shorter and thicker. So, the length and tension of the vocal folds dictate how high or low we phonate (make sound with our voices). The muscles of the larynx are responsible for stretching and relaxing the vocal folds as needed. Did you notice that when she breathed, the vocal folds automatically opened? That is, in fact, the natural resting position of the larynx when we're not making sound. Can you visualize this happening in your very own throat as you read this now? When we breathe, the vocal folds are open. If you're not making sound right now, your vocal folds are resting apart from one another, allowing for inhalation and silent exhalation. When we speak or sing, they close. (Singers often discuss having a good vocal 'closure'.) If you like, click on the short links again to examine and verify these points. Here is another fascinating look inside the human instrument at the level of the vocal cords, as cameras are inserted through the noses and down the throats of four singers - 2 men and 2 women - as they sing in four-part harmony: 0030/THEORY

30 Vocal Cords up close while singing

What an incredible organ! With so many pairs of intrinsic and extrinsic muscles, and an intricate and complex design which enables it to lengthen, shorten, tilt in various ways, this small organ is a marvel.

Now that you've seen how the vocal folds work inside the larynx - how they stretch and tighten for higher pitches, how they get thicker and more relaxed for lower pitches, how they move apart automatically when we breathe - I'd like to suggest a visualization. As you watch and listen to the following clip of famed coloratura soprano **Natalie Dessay** in concert, I'd ask you to simultaneously envision what must be happening in her larynx as she sings. Can you imagine how quickly and precisely her larynx is operating to create those pitches? Can you see it in your mind's eye? Imagine how a stroboscopy might look. (I recommend listening up to at least 1:35 at which point the introduction moves into the main part of the aria. Feel free to enjoy it till the end, of course.)

40 Natalie Dessay - "Où va la jeune Hindoue"

0040/SINGER

The sound you just heard came from a source no bigger than a dime! (or smaller than a 2-cent piece for Europeans). Female vocal folds are between 1.25 and 1.75 cm (approximately 0.5" to 0.75") in length. Adult male vocal folds are between 1.75 and 2.5 cm (approximately 0.75" to 1.0" in length) or about the diameter of an American nickel. An incredibly tiny source to produce all that magnificent sound.

But obviously it takes more than vocal folds to produce sound. What else is needed? How does this human instrument of ours coordinate in order to speak and sing? What are its parts? How do those parts function together? The following links will bring you a long way to understanding how the voice works.

Here's a thorough and entertaining explanation of how the voice works. Different analogies can be used to explain vocal production. In this case, “the voice is like a car”! 0050/THEORY

Let's sum up what we've learned from the last link: the voice has three major components that work together to produce sound in both speech and singing.

1) The breath is our '***fuel***'. It is regulated by the muscles that expand and contract to move air in and out of our lungs, through our windpipe and up to the level of

2) the vocal folds which are housed in the larynx and are the '***sound source***' or 'vibrator'. Then, the sound waves that are produced by the vocal folds vibrating together are filtered through the *vocal tract* which is our voice's

3) '***resonator***'. Without this resonant space our voice wouldn't sound as it does, just as the *inner shape, 'tubing'* or *hollow* of an instrument such as a guitar, violin or drum contributes to its particular sound quality.

In addition, we have a fourth component to help us form words which require not only *vowels* (A, E, I, O, U, and sometimes Y in English) but also *consonants* (B, C, D, F, G, etc.) So, we have

4) 'the ***articulators***', which are the *teeth, tongue* and *lips*, and are responsible for creating consonants which help shape our

60 How the Voice works

words and give them meaning. Click here for a concise written explanation of basic vocal production provided by the *American Academy of Otolaryngology*: 0060/TEXT

Here is another video clip explaining some of the mechanics of voice, including a narration as a stroboscope is lowered into the subject's mouth, down past the epiglottis where it reaches the vocal folds. This clip is entitled, “Fantastic Voyage – a journey into the human voice”. The clip is from a relatively old television program and the quality isn't the best here, but the information is good: 0070/THEORY

70 Fantastic Voyage - a journey into the voice

07 Looking Inside a Few Famous Throats

How about looking into a 'famous throat'? National Geographic created a series called “Incredible Human Machine”, which includes a segment about the voice. Here, **Steven Tyler,** lead singer of the rock Band “Aerosmith", is outfitted with special monitoring equipment by **Dr. Steven Zeitels**, so that we can glimpse the inner workings of his larynx in real-time, performing in front of thousands of people. (Watch from 0:00 to 6:30): 0080/SINGER

80 Incredible Human Machine

90 Roger Daltrey (The Who) and Dr. Zeitels on CBS

Dr. Steven Zeitels is a 'rock star' voice doctor in his own right to many famous pop and rock singers, including Steven Tyler (of 'Aerosmith'), Cher, Lionel Ritchie, Adele, and **Roger Daltry** (of 'The Who'): Here's a news spot about Daltry's vocal struggles and what sent him to seek the help of Dr. Zeitels: 0090/REPORT

Among Zeitel's clients are not only popular music singers, but also world-class opera singers like soprano Carol Vaness, mezzosopranos Denyce Graves and Frederica von Stade among many others. He is also perhaps most noted for helping legendary singer **Julie Andrews** after a botched surgery which was intended to remove non-cancerous growths from her vocal folds. The surgery left her with scarring on her vocal folds which in effect, halted her singing career prematurely. Over the next years Julie Andrews became so invested in Zeitel's work, that she became the honorary chairperson of 'The Voice Restoration Project'.

100 Julie talking about the loss of her voice

How precious these vocal folds are to singers! Here, in an interview with Barbara Walters, Julie Andrews discusses her heartbreaking loss of her voice: 0100/INTERVIEW

Years later after working with Zeitels, Julie Andrews chairs 'The Voice Restoration Project'. In this conference, the latest scientific breakthroughs in creating artificial vocal folds are presented. Zeitels' team has created a 'vocal cord bio-gel' that mimics the action of real vocal folds. The entire talk is interesting and shows how such innovation can also benefit non-singers who have suffered vocal injury. If you wish to jump ahead to see this artificial vocal cord tissue, skip to 8:46: 0110/REPORT

110 Restoring Lost Voices- MGH Voice

Here is Julie Andrews during her heyday, singing 'The Sound of Music' (1972): 0120/SINGER

120 JULIE ANDREWS "THE SOUND OF MUSIC"

The study of voice and singing goes far beyond any anatomy lesson, but it is, after all, our body which is the instrument! A guitarist is interested in knowing a guitar: the body of the instrument, the neck, the strings, the bridge, the tuners, how they operate and combine to create the sound that they love. I would say that it is the same for the singer.

As a beginning classical voice student I had almost no idea how the voice worked, although I had lessons and spent every day practicing. Later, after having acquired this information over the years and as a lecturer at the University of Massachusetts working with undergraduate students, I encountered the same phenomenon among my students. Many voice students didn't know what the larynx was or how the voice functioned. *(This is, in fact, one of the reasons I put together this book! Singers who were never taught it, are often embarrassed to ask basic questions about how the voice works and basic vocal anatomy.)* But much seems to be changing in the area of vocal study and students are getting more information earlier on. There are some amazing institutions which are very advanced indeed, and take this aspect of a singer's education seriously. One of these is Oberlin University in Ohio where I was lucky enough to attend the Symposium for Voice Performance and Pedagogy under the leadership of renowned tenor and scholar Richard Miller who was a pioneer in this area and authored many books and hundreds of articles on the subject of voice and singing. At Oberlin University, students can monitor their progress as vocalists using the scientific instrumentation in the Otto B. Schoepfle Vocal Arts Laboratory.

130 Otto B. Schoepfle Vocal Arts Laboratory

Click here for a description of the voice laboratory equipment and purpose of such analyses: 0130/TEXT

The following link entitled 'Visualizing the Operatic Voice' is a presentation that was given at Oberlin University as part of the Chicago Humanities Festival. It contains a tremendous amount of useful information about how and why singers sound the way they sound with the main focus being on opera singers, although there is also discussion of 'non-classical' singing. Included are live demonstrations which are analyzed in real-time, using visual and auditory technology as well as analyses of famous singers. (If you are new to singing or even if you're a seasoned singer you might find this presentation a bit on the academic side. Don't worry about understanding everything right away! If you're just beginning, let this be an opportunity to simply be exposed to some new topics and ideas. You can also let your curiosity roam...for example, do you agree - as proposed in the introduction - that in service of their art, opera singers are 'singing athletes'?) Feel free to skip around and listen to small portions rather than the entire lecture. If, on the other hand, you find this sort of analysis engaging, feel free to enjoy the hour-long presentation: 0140/PRESENT

140 Visualizing the Operatic Voice

But is science and state-of-the-art equipment really necessary for great singing? Of course not. Singing and excellence in singing predates any need for such modern apparatus and scientific analyses, however, the use of such equipment *can* indeed enhance a singer's understanding of their vocal production and help to change or improve it. What is undeniable though, is that modern technology is of great advantage in diagnosing and treating voice problems.

08 Overtone Singing

Doc-Number/ LinkList 2 : ***34718-5583***

But now for something completely different. Do you know who probably hasn't seen the inside of a voice laboratory and is, nevertheless, a great singer? Here, a female Mongolian '*throat singer*' shares her rich vocal tradition. If you hear more than one tone emanating from the voice of this impressive singer, you aren't hallucinating, nor is there someone simultaneously playing a small flute somewhere off-stage!

After a few opening lines the singer will produce a fundamental pitch and then you will be able to hear a whistle-like melody floating above that one (listen for it at 1:10). In essence, two vocal lines can be heard at the same time.

This type of singing is called '***overtone singing***', '***throat singing***' or '***harmonic singing***', and there are dozens of styles and traditions throughout the world. Overtone singing is thought to have originated in south western Mongolia, and the region is still likely the most active place of overtone singing in the world. In this style, the singer trains to achieve a fundamental or 'base note' that has a sustained, guttural, deep and pressurized quality which then provides an even greater contrast to the flute-like overtones that are created above this fundamental pitch. You may be surprised that this is indeed a woman singing! 0150/SINGER

150 Female Mongolian Throat Singer

If a singer can produce two pitches at the same time does this mean that they have special anatomy which is different to yours and mine? No. In overtone singing, a single, fundamental pitch is produced by the vocal folds vibrating (as in all traditions of singing) but then the singer is able to select and amplify certain 'overtones' and this occurs in the resonant cavities of the *mouth*, the *nasal cavities,* the *larynx* and the *pharynx.* (The *pharynx* is a cone-shaped passageway which extends all along down from the level of the nose, the mouth, and down to the level of the larynx. These specific areas are called, respectively, *the nasopharynx, the oropharynx* and *the laryngopharynx.*) By making small and precise adjustments to, for example, the tongue placement, the shape of the inside of the mouth and nasal cavities, and by changing the vowels, the overtone singer can then enhance certain natural overtones, while blocking off others, thereby giving the *impression* that they are singing two separate pitches.

To understand how someone can appear to make two pitches at once, we need to know that sound waves made by the human voice are made from, not only *one* absolute pitch, but also 'overtones'.

A good comparison here is the phenomenon of light. Consider how sunlight, when refracted, actually reveals various wavelengths that have different colours - as in, all the colours of the rainbow. When light is filtered in a certain way, certain colours seem to appear before our eyes, like in the case of a sunset. Light is always made up of a combination of these colours to produce what we ordinarily see as 'white light', but under certain circumstances selected elements of this white light come to the foreground, so to speak, and we see a particular colour or colours.

It's the same with the voice. We perceive one sound, one pitch, but it actually contains a rainbow of tones that exist above that fundamental tone - hence the term 'overtone'. We don't ordinarily hear these overtones as separate from the fundamental tone, but they're there. Overtone singers play with overtones to a magical effect.

160 Polyphonic overtone singing - explained visually

Here is an excellent visual explanation and demonstration of overtone singing by **Anna-Maria Hefele**. There is a spectrogram, which is a visual representation of the voice, and also a keyboard on the side of the screen so you can picture exactly what you are hearing: 0160/PRESENT

170 Seven Styles of Overtone Singing (Tuvan Throat Singing)

Here's an amazing display of 7 styles of ***Tuvan throat singing***. Pay attention to how this young man makes very subtle and precise movements of his mouth, tongue and internal resonances. Listen for the 'whistle-like' melody that can be heard separately from the fundamental tone: 0170/SINGER

Inspired to give it a try yourself? Here Anna-Maria Hefele shares hints on how to get started with overtone singing.

Here are Part 1 and 2 of Anna-Maria Hefele's mini-tutorial on overtone singing: 0180/LESSON **** 0190/LESSON

190 Overtone singing-2: by Anna-Maria Hefele

180 Overtone singing- l: by Anna-Maria Hefele

Some styles of throat singing focus less on overtones and more on guttural fundamental pitches and rhythmic breathing. There is a resurgence of the Inuit tradition of ***Katajjaq,*** in which the performers are typically two women who participate in this type of friendly competition to see who can outlast the other, or who will be the first to laugh.

Here, **Tanya Tagaq** from Nunavut, Canada, explains and demonstrates this style of throat singing. The next clip provides a little more insight into the tradition of *Katajjaq* throat singing, and shows 2 sisters in a 'duet'. 0200/LESSON **** 0210/SINGER

09 Yodeling: Overtone Singing's Kissin' Cousin

Most people are somewhat familiar with *yodeling*, which might be considered a cousin of overtone singing. In yodeling, specific overtones are not selected, but rather, the singer quickly and repeatedly switches between low 'chest voice' register and higher, 'head voice' or 'falsetto' register. (Later on we'll look at what some of these terms mean.) The singer may change registers several times in only a few seconds at a high volume. It is thought that yodeling developed in the central Alps by herders calling to their flocks. ***Franzl Lang*** is known as the 'Yodel King' (*Jodlerkönig)* from Bavaria in Germany. In the next link you will hear a sample of what he can do. In the subsequent link, you'll hear a young American girl

230 Awesome Yodeling - 12 year old Yodel

220 Yodelling - Franzl Lang

wow the judges on a popular television talent show with her yodeling. It's believed that yodeling was brought over to America by German immigrants in Pennsylvania in the early 1800's. 0220/YODEL **** 0230/YODEL

10 Resonance and the Vocal Tract

We've seen that the *vocal tract* is the cavity where the sound emanating from the vibration of the vocal folds is *filtered*, thereby giving the voice its specific characteristics and qualities. Without resonance, the sound of the vocal folds vibrating alone would be nothing more than a thin buzzing sound. The length and thickness of the vocal folds only partially determine the quality of sound. It's really the vocal tract that is responsible for amplifying and mellowing the sound. (The voice can also partially resonate in the chest cavity, but does primarily in the vocal tract.)

The vocal tract can be viewed as the 'tubing' of the human vocal instrument. The estimated average length of the adult male vocal tract is about 16.9 cm and 14.1 cm for adult females. It consists of the laryngeal cavity, the pharynx, the oral cavity (mouth) and the nasal cavities and sinuses – essentially, the passageway with all its nooks and crannies from your vocal folds all the way through to your mouth. Consider how the quality of your own voice changes when you are 'stuffed up' from a cold, or when your sinuses are blocked. This can give you some insight into the importance of resonance to produce a certain quality of sound.

In the next link you'll be able to actually view the 'inside' of someone singing with the help of an MRI - and specifically, you'll be able to see the vocal tract in real-time. Here, the subjects are a female opera singer and a male beatboxer. Pay attention to the dark areas - that is, the *space* or *tubing* where the sound waves that are formed at the vocal folds are then able to resonate. You'll notice that the whole area can be quite dynamic, especially the movement of the tongue being responsible for changing the shape within the vocal tract to help create the various vowels. Yes, tongues are *that* big! We normally only see the tip. (Note: there is some distortion at the top of the soprano's voice due to the difficult conditions of sound recording in a real-time MRI. Also, there is a dark spot which occasionally appears in the middle of the soprano's tongue – this is *not* a hole or a strange, loop-shaped tongue! The dark spot appears in the MRI due to some dental work that the subject has had.)

235 The diva and the emcee

0235/PRESENT

Here is a more recent and excellent quality MRI of a male opera singer singing a Wagner aria. Observe the vocal tract and the movement of the tongue. Can you see that the singer seems to utilize the vocal tract a bit differently than the beatboxer we've just seen? There appears to be more 'space'...that is, the larynx seems to be slightly lower and all the resonant chambers remain a little more 'open', for longer. You may notice the more precise movements of the tongue to create the vowels.

240 MRI

0240/PRESENT

11 Voice Impressions

Have you ever wondered why each person has such a distinct and recognizable voice? To some degree it has to do with the thickness and length of the vocal folds, but in very large part, the shape of the vocal tract is responsible for their individual and particular sound. Just as we can recognize different people due to the shape of their face and the shape of the features on their face, their voice is also molded by their 'inside shape' and becomes similarly recognizable to us. A person's size and their bone structure will also give their sound a certain *timbre*, or 'vocal colour'.

Voice impressionists mimic other peoples' mannerisms, accents and speech patterns, but first and foremost, they try to recreate their vocal timbre. To a great degree, they do this by playing with resonance. They purposely change 'their inside shape'. For example, they might move their larynx up or down, change the shape and opening of their mouth, jut their jaw forward or pull it back, change the position of their tongue or direct the resonance to be more or less *nasal* (focused 'in the nose') or they might try to focus the resonance in the back of the throat to make it darker or more 'woofy'. Intuitively, and with lots of practice, these impressionists are temporarily altering the shape of their own vocal tract to resemble the vocal tract of another person. Quite a remarkable and complex undertaking when you think about it. In this clip, **Christina Bianco** does impressions of famous female vocalists. Personally, I find her Celine Dion and Barbra Streisand impressions excellent, and her Adele and Cher impressions not as good. Among the other singers she mimics are:
Judy Garland, Alanis Morissette, Kristin Chenoweth, Edith Piaf,

Bette Midler, Julie Andrews, Liza Minnelli, Bernadette Peters, Gwen Stefani, Zooey Deschanel, Britney Spears, Shakira, Norah Jones and Christina Aguilera. Can you recognise the voices? Then, in the second video, impressionist **Jim Meskimen** recites an essay on what qualities reside in a human voice, but he does it using 38 different celebrity impressions. See how many voices you can recognize! 0250/PERFORM

250 Christina Bianco Diva Impressions 'Total Eclipse Of The

**** 0260/PERFORM

260 What Is In a Human Voice?

In a series of instructional videos aimed to help those interested in improving their impressionist skills, Jim Meskimen shares some tips. In this - Part 7 - he encourages you to "play with your face". 0270/PRESENT

270 How To Do Impressions

12 More on Resonance: Western vs. Chinese Opera

Perhaps you're already familiar with the sound of Chinese Opera and the very different sound of Western Opera. (If not, you'll get a chance to hear both styles in the links below.) We've already looked at how the voice functions. Now let's see if we can determine why Chinese opera and Western opera sound so different, vocally speaking.

Chinese opera predates Western opera by over half a

millennium, and has its own musical style, instrumentation, customs in face-painting, character types, costumes, story lines, dance, martial arts and acrobatics, which are all very different to what constitutes Western opera. Chinese opera is an amalgamation of many art forms which has evolved over more than a thousand years. Singers study its particular vocal style and train for years to perfect the sound and vocal timbre that is favoured for this art form.

In the West, opera has flourished since the 16th century in Europe, with precursors of the art form developing hundreds of years before that. Western opera is similar to Chinese opera in that it is essentially also a dramatic work combining text and music (singers and musicians) and generally also has acting, costuming and scenery. The vocal style for Western opera has evolved differently, however. The preferred Western operatic sound is very different from the preferred Chinese operatic sound.

Let's have a look at two clips. Pay attention to the difference in vocal timbre, and imagine what might be happening in terms of *resonance* and vocal function in each case.
Afterwards let's contrast the Chinese operatic performance with Western operatic sound. What differences in sound can you perceive? Here is **Shengsu Li**, a star of the Beijing Opera, and afterwards, dramatic soprano **Eva Marton** singing 'In questa reggia' from Puccini's opera *Turandot*.

0280/SINGER **** 0290/SINGER

Now that you've heard examples of both, do you have a preference? To western ears Chinese opera can sound shrill and pinched. The Chinese operatic vocal tradition has simply evolved to favour this type of sound. (It's been speculated that the sound is evocative of and compliments some of the Chinese orchestral instruments.) Western operatic vocal timbre is not everyone's cup of tea either! Many people prefer a more intimate, 'speech-like' vocalism, as in jazz or contemporary popular music. There is no right or wrong here.

To westerners, the defining characteristic of Chinese operatic singing is *nasality.* The singer creates a resonant effect that strives to achieve a 'high-pitched tone'. He or she focuses resonance in the nasal cavity, sinuses and the front portion of the face (sometimes referred to by singers as *the mask*). In contrast, the Western operatic sound also exploits space in the 'back parts' of the vocal tract which creates a darker effect. Westerners don't seem to favour the Chinese type of extreme forward 'placement' and rather seek to create a sound that has bright elements as well as dark elements. This is typically referred to as ***chiaroscuro*** and exists in the visual art world as well. It is an Italian term that means 'light-dark' or 'bright-dark'. The contrast of these elements creates the impression of fullness and three-dimensionalism. In this way, Chinese operatic sound would be considered to be much more on the 'chiaro' (light, or bright) side, and much less on the 'scuro' (dark) side. The Western operatic sound rather seeks a balance of the two. (If you missed it the first time, listen again to see if you can perceive the *chiaroscuro* balance in the Puccini aria. You should easily be able to identify a fuller, darker sound in the Puccini aria as opposed to the brightness and nasality of the Chinese opera.)

13 Being heard over an orchestra

Doc-Number/LinkList 3 : ***34718-6477***

In Western opera (from now on we'll use 'opera' to refer to the Western tradition and not the Chinese tradition), singers exploit resonance in a different way. A seemingly mysterious characteristic of operatic singing is the ability of the singer's voice to be heard above even large orchestras. Does this mean that opera singers are simply louder than all of the orchestral instruments combined? No. Although some operatic voices can indeed produce a lot of volume, it is more a phenomenon of *resonance.* The human vocal tract produces various acoustic resonances which are referred to as ***formants***. Vocalizations almost always have 4 to 6 distinguishable formants with the first two formants (*F1* and *F2*) being responsible for determining pitch (how high or low a note is) and vowel quality (in English, simplified: A,E,I,O,U and sometimes Y).

Beyond this, particularly in male operatic voices – tenors, baritones and basses – there exists the phenomenon of the ***'Singer's formant'***, which is a clustering together of formants 3, 4, and 5. The Singer's formant produces a sort of 'ring' and amplification effect that cuts through orchestras. According to expert Dr. Johan Sundberg, it is - in very basic terms - *achieved by having a low larynx and a wide pharyngeal position in singing*. It's important to remember, however, that s*inging is always a dynamic interplay and coordination of breath management, phonation and resonance balancing and adjusting. No single, static posture of the larynx and pharynx is ever 'the whole story'.*

Female opera singers can produce the Singer's formant as well, but it is generally less common. Sundberg believes this is due to the female vocal tract being too short to achieve the necessary clustering of formants. Other vocal scientists would dispute this as the reason for female operatic voices not achieving the Singer's formant as regularly. In any case, the higher pitches that female operatic singers sing, along with vibrant and unrestricted overtones present, is often enough for them to also be heard over the orchestra.

Italian opera singer **Luciano Pavarotti** was one of the finest tenors of the 20th century and as fine an example of a singer to have mastered the Singer's formant as could be. See if you can perceive the 'ring' and presence to his sound which is audible whether he is singing loudly or quietly. (In later years, Pavarotti's concerts were held in huge stadiums and other such large venues so that microphones were used both for him and the orchestra. In an opera house his voice could be easily heard over the orchestra without any such amplification.) Here he is, singing the famous aria 'Nessun Dorma' from Puccini's opera *Turandot*. 0300/SINGER

300 Pavarotti - Nessun Dorma

In a 1981 interview, Pavarotti reveals some of his thoughts about performing: the challenges of singing in different acoustic environments, how small fluctuations in the voice on any given day can affect singing, how a high C is like shooting a goal in soccer, and singing with famed Australian soprano Dame Joan Sutherland. He uses musical terms such as *bel canto* (literally translated from the Italian as 'beautiful singing' or 'beautiful song', but it can also refer to a certain singing tradition and to certain operas of the 18th and early 19th centuries – for more information on *bel canto* click on the Wiki-link: 0310/TEXT). He also uses the terms *legato* (an Italian term which means the notes are sung or played in a smooth, connected way, 'tied together') and the term *coloratura* (an Italian term which literally means 'colouring' and refers to virtuosic singing in operatic repertoire which includes vocal runs, trills and leaps): 0320/INTERV

310 Wikipedia Bel Canto

320 Luciano Pavarotti Interview

Here is Pavarotti discussing another legendary Italian operatic tenor, **Franco Corelli.** It's interesting to get his perspective on Corelli's voice and career, the influence of television on building superstars, and to hear Pavarotti's admiration for Corelli: 0330/INTERV Here is Franco Corelli in concert, singing the famous aria which Pavarotti mentions in the above interview, 'Che gelida manina' from Puccini's *La Boheme.* Corelli was dubbed 'the Prince of Tenors'. Can you appreciate his mastery of *chiaroscuro* and can you perceive the 'ring' in the voice that is likely the *Singer's formant* in all its glory? (In the next clip you will hear Pavarotti singing the same aria, so pay attention to Corelli's

330 Pavarotti about Franco Corelli

340 Franco Corelli "Che gelida manina"

quality, his vocal timbre, so you can then compare.) 0340/SINGER

Here's Pavarotti singing the same aria except this time it is not a concert version but rather an excerpt from the opera itself, with costumes, movement and acting. Of course this automatically makes it a different experience from a concert setting, but this aside - as you listen, you might ask yourself who you prefer, or do you like them equally? Whose voice is darker, stronger, sweeter, brighter? Both these operatic tenors were technical masters, displayed excellent *chiaroscuro* and *Singer's formant,* but there are differences in the voices. ***These two tenors are not considered the same TYPE of tenor, although they are singing the same aria here. A little later we will look at the various operatic voice types, and what that means.*** For now, try to find out for yourself what qualities you like and what moves you most about the performances. And do you like the drama and movement of the opera, or do you prefer the concert version? There are no right answers and you don't even need to prefer one over another - simply pay attention to how you respond: 0350/SINGER

350 Che gelida manina - Luciano Pavarotti

14 Attention Voice Nerds!

For those of you who are more scientifically minded and would like to understand more about the 'science of voice' - *formants* and acoustic principles of the human voice - the following four links will be enlightening. Some singers and singing teachers who are very interested in this type of information have been affectionately referred to, or refer to themselves as, 'voice nerds'.

(For those of you who are less interested in the science and more in the artistry of singing, please feel free to skip over the next four clips to 'Opera Singers: On-stage and Off-stage.)

To better understand the concept of *formants,* here is a wonderful mini-lecture explaining the first two formants – 'the vowel formants' - *F1* and *F2.* (The 'Singer's formant' is not touched upon in this clip): 0360/PRESENT

The following clip is a nice explanation given by singing teacher Karyn O'Connor, about resonance, formants and harmonics, and how and why singers adjust these for optimal sound production. She mentions that 'singers are primarily artists and not academics', but a knowledge of what's happening with your instrument can indeed bring your singing to the next level. After having learned some of the terminology in previous sections, you should be able to follow much of what is presented here: 0370/PRESENT

360 Where do formants come from ?

370 VOCAL FORMANTS AND HARMONICS Explained!

Here is a lecture given by Dr. Johan Sundberg. He is a preeminent scholar, acoustician and renowned for his work on the acoustical properties of the human voice. This is a somewhat dry, academic and scientific analysis of the voice as a musical instrument and, unfortunately, the video quality here isn't very good, but there is a treasure trove of information for those wishing to delve into the science of voice. At 20:49 he discusses the Singer's formant and you can hear an example of the difference in sound, with and without the Singer's formant present against a backdrop of noise which could be comparable to the wall of sound an orchestra can produce. It's remarkable how the Singer's formant cuts through the noise while without the Singer's formant, the vocal line gets lost. Some of the information presented here is rather advanced, so feel free to watch short segments or skip right to the discussion on Singer's formant. (As a point of interest, as Dr. Sundberg became more and more interested in the acoustics of voice he began his own vocal journey and gave his first public song recital on his 50th birthday.) 0380/PRESENT

380 Prof. Johan Sundberg

Have you ever wondered what made Pavarotti so great? Many years after his death singers are still analyzing what he was able to to do. Here is a post from Jean-Ronald LaFond's blog 'Kashu-do, The Way of the Singer'. This post is entitled "Pavarotti's Legacy: Efficient Phonation or the baby's cry". (After reading, you can then link to dozens of other blog posts and take a sneak peek into the issues opera singers and singing teachers are talking about. There is a tremendous amount of information covered in this blog.) 0390/TEXT

390 The Way of the Singer

15 Opera Singers: On-stage and off-stage

Some opera singers have achieved such extraordinary vocal virtuosity and attained such mastery in performance that it seems almost super-human. A few female opera singers have been hailed 'diva', which means 'goddess'. This term is wide-spread today and is commonly used for popular singers and entertainers, but decades ago it was reserved for only the most exceptionally accomplished female operatic singers. ('Divo' is the equivalent for men, but this term never caught on in the same way, although some male operatic singers have also certainly reached 'superstar' status.)

The following clips are a *small* sampling of some extraordinary operatic singers. Every generation has had their opera superstars. Some are the stuff of legend, since recording technology in the early days was primitive, or not yet available. The following is no way meant to be a comprehensive overview of history's most famous and/or influential opera singers, as this would require another, or several other books. Rather, here we can marvel at few singers' virtuosity, their artistry and also get an inside glimpse of them as people via interviews, 'vlogs' (video blogs), or in masterclasses as they guide and teach prospective young singers.

Joyce DiDonato is a world-renowned American **mezzo-soprano** who began her professional career in 1998/99. She is splendid on stage and happens to also produce a 'vlog' called 'Yankee Diva', where she responds to questions from fans and aspiring singers. She regularly gives masterclasses where she imparts some of her own experience and vocal wisdom to the next, up-and-coming generation of opera singers.

400 Rossini: Non più mesta (La Cenerentola) - DiDonato

Here is Joyce DiDonato in concert, singing 'Non piu mesta' from the opera *La Cenerentola* by Rossini, replete with *coloratura* – the Italian term which means elaborate vocal lines - runs, trills, leaps and other vocal acrobatics.

0400/SINGER

Joyce DiDonato's 'Vlog' - 'The Yankee Diva': 'That persistent, inner voice'. Here, Ms. Donato shares her ideas and experience on self-sabotaging thoughts and self-criticism which might hinder good performance. It's intriguing to hear a singer at the top of her game sharing openly and honestly about her own insecurities and how she's come to deal with that aspect of being an artist.

410 That persistent, inner voice

0410/VLOG

The following is a clip of a Joyce DiDonato masterclass given at the Guildhall School of Music and Drama in London. Watch her guide and inspire a young soprano to sing 'Caro nome' from Verdi's *Rigoletto.* She uses unconventional means to draw out a deeper dramatic interpretation from the young artist.

420 Joyce DiDonato Vocal Masterclass

0420/MCLASS

Famed American **baritone *Thomas Hampson*** began his stellar career in the early 1980's. His career has included not only singing performance but also music scholarship and education.

You'll now hear Thomas Hampson sing Korngold's 'Mein Sehnen, mein Wähnen' from the opera *Die tote Stadt,* in concert. Following that, Mr. Hampson leads a masterclass and guides a young Chinese baritone in singing the same aria. Finally, you'll hear him giving advice to young people who would like to pursue a career in music.

430 Thomas Hampson sings Korngold

440 Thomas Hampson Voice Masterclass

0430/SINGER

0440/MCLASS

**** 0450/NARRAT

450 How Not to Fail At Opera

Internationally acclaimed Russian **soprano *Anna Netrebko*** began her career in the early 1990's and has since established herself as one of the world's most sought-after opera singers.

460 Anna Netrebko - Casta Diva (Norma)

Here Anna Netrebko sings Bellini's 'Casta Diva' from the opera *Norma,* in concert. (For those of you eager to get to the singing and want to skip over the orchestral introduction, you can jump ahead to 1:35.) 0460/SINGER

Before we look at Ms. Netrebko's video blog and see an excerpt from a documentary about her, we will listen to perhaps the most famous soprano of all time - Maria Callas - singing the same aria, 'Casta Diva'. Here is an opportunity for you to, once again, compare these two interpretations and the differences in qualities of voice. Callas' voice and career were controversial. She was a huge celebrity in her time and countless books have been written about her life and artistry. Some consider her sound 'an acquired taste', others argue that she was *the* quintessential opera singer. But without a doubt, she is legendary. If you haven't heard her before and you become intrigued, there is no shortage of recordings, Youtube links, documentaries and books about Callas who was called not only called 'diva' but hailed 'La Divina' - 'the Divine One'. 0470/SINGER

470 Casta Diva (Maria Callas)

Now let's get back to Ms. Netrebko. She happens to also have a video blog called 'Ask Anna' where she answers fan mail. Here, she talks about her high notes, eating before a performance, singing and acting, and dealing with criticism. 0480/NARRAT **** 0490/NARRAT **** 500/NARRAT **** 0510/NARRAT

There are dozens of full-length interviews and documentaries about Anna Netrebko. Here is an excerpt of

one such documentary where we get a glimpse into her daily professional and personal life. Please take note of the commentator's remarks about ***voice type.*** He states that it is an opera singer's *range* and *quality* that determine what operatic roles they will sing. Netrebko herself states that she is a *lyric soprano*, so that her voice is suited to certain operatic roles, often those of young girls. But voices can change over time! She mentions that she may be moving into more dramatic roles in the future. (As mentioned before, there will be further discussion about *voice type* a little later on.) Let's find out a bit more about Ms. Netrebko now.
0520/NARRAT

520 Anna Netrebko Documentary Part 2

German opera singer ***Jonas Kaufmannn*** began his career in 1994 and has since become one of the world's leading **tenors**. We've heard, Pavarotti and Corelli sing it, and now we will hear the same aria for a 3rd time. Yet another opportunity to compare and contrast voices and performances, in addition to getting to know the beautiful aria 'Che gelida manina' from Puccini's opera *La Boheme,* more deeply. Here is Jonas Kaufmannn in a recording session for Decca Records.
0530/SINGER

530 Jonas Kaufmannn: "Che gelida manina"

In the next clip Mr. Kaufmannn talks about how it took him some time early on in his career to really discover the natural capabilities of his tenor voice. He mentions his initial vocal uncertainties and difficulties at the start of his career and how

540 Interview
Jonas Kaufmann

he had to make radical changes in order to take command of his instrument. He discusses his international success and his hopes for the future. 0540/INTERV

550 Interview

In this interview, Mr. Kaufmannn discusses his recording of *verismo* arias. He describes how in this operatic style the voice is the pure transporter of emotions, and that the intention is not necessarily to create the most gorgeous sound if it does not serve to transmit these emotions. 0550/INTERV

16 Voice Categorization – What the *Fach*?

Doc-Number/LinkList 4 : ***34718-8534***

In the clips above, you heard examples of a mezzo-soprano, a baritone, 2 sopranos and a tenor. Some of you may already have an idea of what these terms mean, and some of you may not.

Traditionally, in choral repertoire (choir music) the situation is quite clear and that's a good place to start when trying to understand voice categorization. In the most common configuration of choirs, women are categorized into *soprano* and *alto*, while the men sing *tenor* and *bass*: SATB. Sopranos generally sing the highest pitches, with the alto line below them. The male tenors then sing below the female altos, and the basses sing the lowest pitches.

This might lead us to believe that voice categorization depends entirely on how high or low a voice can sing, but this is only part of the story. Vocal categorization can become quite complex in the operatic world.

Many factors are at play in determining the categorization of a voice. The word '***Fach***' was used by German opera houses in the 19th century to help describe voices, which would aid in auditioning and casting roles. *Fach* (the 'ch' is pronounced with a throaty 'h' rather than a typical 'ch' in English) is a German word which has various meanings, including 'compartment' and 'shelf'. In the operatic sense, *Fach* really refers to voice 'category' or 'type' and the term is widespread and still used today.

Earlier we heard 3 different operatic tenors - Luciano Pavarotti, Franco Corelli and Jonas Kaufmann singing the same Puccini aria, 'Che gelida manina'. It's likely you could perceive differences in their sound. (If you didn't, feel free to double back and listen again.) The differences in timbre are there because although they are all tenor voices, Pavarotti was a *lyric tenor,* Corelli was a *spinto tenor* and Kaufmann is sometimes considered something in between! In the links below you will discover what these terms mean. Sometimes singers don't even fit easily into one particular *Fach* and their abilities lie outside those parameters. Opera aficionados sometimes disagree and debate the *Fach* of a particular singer.

So, what are the different operatic voice types, or *Fächer*? The three primary categories of female operatic voices from 'highest to lowest' are: *soprano, mezzosoprano,* and *contralto.*

The male operatic voice types from 'highest to lowest' are: *tenor, baritone* and *bass.* So far, so good - only six in total. However, at this point there are further subcategories.

Here are the main subcategories of the *soprano* voice: *Soubrette, Lyric Coloratura, Dramatic Coloratura, Light Lyric, Lyric, Spinto/Young Dramatic, Dramatic*. All of them sopranos! Mezzos, contraltos and the male voices also have their own subcategories. So, what factors help determine someone's *Fach*? There are many, and *range* (the notes your body can produce from lowest to highest) is only one factor. In fact, some voice types' ranges can overlap. But what is the 'colour' of the voice? Dark? Light? Warm? Dramatic or steely? What are its particular attributes? Is the voice very agile and does it like to move, or is it heavier and more powerful? Is the voice more comfortable sitting for longer periods of time in the upper part of their range or not? These are only some of the considerations that help determine *Fach*. The following article decribes twenty-five voice types in the *Fach* system and provides a comprehensive chart of these, along with a description of some of the characteristics that they generally exhibit.

560 The Fach-System

0560/TEXT

With all these voice types you'd think that every voice would easily fall into one category. In fact, some voices cross over into two or more categories, or change with age, development and experience. World-famous tenor Placido Domingo began as a baritone and later discovered he was, in fact, a large-voiced tenor. There are countless stories of singers discovering their 'true *Fach*' later on in their careers, or voices evolving through many *Fächer* over the course of their careers, typically moving into heavier and more dramatic repertoire over time. Do you remember Anna Netrebko in an earlier clip, mentioning that after her son was born her voice seemed to get bigger? She was considering transitioning into more *dramatic* repertoire and leaving the *lyric* repertoire, as the critics were suggesting.

I highly recommend checking out this next link. It is an *extremely* helpful resource and provides **recordings of singers of various types** singing excerpts of arias from operatic roles in their *Fach*. You can click on the various excerpts to compare and contrast voice types easily. It also provides a short, written description of each *Fach*. (You'll notice there are yet even more voice types described here, sometimes in Italian terminology rather than their German counterparts). You may be surprised to realize, for example, that sometimes a *dramatic soprano* sounds more like a *mezzo-soprano* than she does a *light lyric* or *soubrette* soprano voice. If you would like to hear the difference between, say, a *dramatic soprano* and a *soubrette* for example, or a *buffo bass* and a *basso profundo*, click here. 0570/DEMO

570 Opera Voices –the basic Fachs

For a more general comparison, let's take a look at three clips. The first is of German soprano ***Diana Damrau***. There is some controversy about her *Fach*. She can sing *soubrette* roles, some *lyric* as well as *coloratura* roles. She is likely not a *dramatic coloratura soprano* as this *Fach* usually requires more 'weight' in the voice. We'll also hear American soprano ***Renée Fleming*** who is a *full lyric soprano*. Finally, we'll hear Italian *coloratura mezzo-soprano* ***Cecilia Bartoli.*** As you listen, can you perceive the differences in the voices although they are singing the same aria? Do these differences match the descriptions of the voice types you've now read about?

Here are the three divas singing the 'Allelujah' from Mozart's famous 'Exultate, Jubilate' K165.

580 Diana Damrau

590 Renée Fleming

600 Cecilia Bartoli

Diana Damrau: 0580/SINGER
Renée Fleming: 0590/SINGER
Cecilia Bartoli: 0600/SINGER

The Lyric Opera of Chicago offers an interesting series of talks on the various voice types. It's an illustrious panel, including famed soprano Renée Fleming whom we’ve just heard, conductor Andrew Davis and the LOC's general director Anthony Freud. You'll not only hear about the various voice types, but also the challenges of certain operatic roles and even some insight into vocal production and technique from Ms. Fleming. As of yet, there is no segment on the *mezzosoprano* voice, but the panel discusses the *baritone, soprano* and *tenor* voice types.

610 Voice types: Baritone

LyricU Presents – Voice types: Baritone: 0610/DEMO

620 Voice types: Soprano

LyricU Presents – Voice types: Soprano: 0620/DEMO

630 Voice types: Tenor

LyricU Presents – Voice types: Tenor: 0630/DEMO

17 The *Countertenor*

A voice type that sometimes surprises people is the *countertenor.* He is also sometimes referred to as a *falsettist.* This is a male voice type whose range is more or less equivalent to that of a female contralto or mezzosoprano's. Actually, these singers are most often natural tenors or even baritones but they have developed their 'falsetto' voices to create a certain sound, often for particular types of music and particular repertory. To read more about this, click on the wiki-link: 0640/WIKI

640
Countertenor

The vocal production of a countertenor is different from other operatic voice types in that the singer's vocal-folds do not come together or 'close' in a typical way while singing. In Richard Miller's book 'The Structure of Singing', he states: "High-speed motion pictures of the larynx during falsetto production reveal that the folds vibrate and come into contact only at the free borders and that the remainder of the folds remains relatively firm and non-vibratory. Furthermore, the folds appear long, stiff, very thin along the edges, and somewhat bow-shaped." (Miller, 1996, p.121) He cites various voice scientists and vocal pedagogues who further describe the mechanics: "The falsetto is sung with only the foremost parts of the cords left free to vibrate at the margins, the rest being damped."(Brodnitz, 1953, p.82)

What does this voice type sound like? The following is a clip of world-famous American countertenor ***David Daniels***.

We also get to hear him interviewed, so we have the opportunity to hear his normal, spoken voice. (By listening to him speak, I would guess that Daniels possesses a natural tenor voice.) In addition, we hear his thoughts on the development of his voice over time, as well as the observations of Harry Bicket, the artistic director of the English Concert, who has worked with Daniels over a number of years. 0650/DEMO

650 David Daniels - Bach

18 World Record for Highest Note Sung by a Man

Adam Lopez realized he had a knack for singing high notes and developed his ability. In the following clip he demonstrates that he can reach a C#8, which is 2 octaves higher than the soprano high C. In his blog 'Kashu-do: The Way of the Singer', vocal pedagogue Jean-Ronald LaFond explains that 'theoretically' Lopez is not a freak! Before watching the Guinness World Record clip, let's read what LaFond has to say about the matter: "Theoretically, there is a finite maximum [vocal-]fold mass and therefore a low pitch limit for any given voice. However, there is an infinite possibility of [vocal-fold] mass reduction and therefore an infinite possibility of high pitch production, "theoretically". The following singer is not a freak, but simply someone who probably had unconsciously developed a facility in the falsetto range which got him attention. As a result, he continued to develop this ability.

The singer sang nearly an octave above his previous record, which proves that coordination improves with training. His final note was C#8, two octaves above the soprano high C and beyond the piano keyboard. The coordination is referred to as *damping*, whereby only a portion of the vocal folds is vibrating (this production is also called *whistle voice*). In essence, the smaller the vibrating portion, the higher the singer can sing. The vibrating portion can be made infinitely smaller and therefore, the pitch level can be theoretically infinitely higher." (LaFond, Kashu-do blog, July 27, 2008)

660 Highest Vocal Note- World Record

Here is Adam Lopez setting the Guinness World Record: 0660/DEMO

19 Where, or where have the Castrati gone?

One voice type that has, perhaps thankfully, disappeared from the classical music world is the male castrato voice. In mid-16th century Europe it became fashionable to groom boys for classical singing careers from an early age. A boy exhibiting talent, or ambitious parents might have had their son undergo castration (surgical removal of the testicles) before he reached the age of puberty. As a result, his prepubescent vocal range would be retained as his larynx would not develop in the usual manner under the influence of the hormones which normally change the shape of the larynx at sexual maturity, thus avoiding the 'dropping' of the voice. Furthermore, a lack of testosterone had the added effect of the limbs growing unusually long, as well as most of the bones, including the ribs.

This, combined with rigorous training gave *castrati* the ability for amazing breath capacity and control, as well as very high notes. (Women and girls were banned from singing in church choirs or on stages which fueled the need for boys to sing the higher parts.)
At the beginning of the 18th century *castrati* were among the most famous and glamorous personalities of their time. They were the 'pop idols' of their day. (The 1994 film by Gérard Corbiau, ***Farinelli,*** is about one such superstar castrato.)

The following several links are the complete 6 parts of the BBC documentary entitled 'Castrato' where you can learn much more about this historical and vocal phenomenon. It is the aim of the producers of this documentary to digitally recreate what a real castrato might have sounded like by taking aspects of various male, female and children's voices and synthesizing them. The castrato voice was said to be 'other-worldly', 'angelic' and 'eerie'. There is discussion of *countertenors, boy sopranos, male altos* as well as some of the female voice types. See what you think of their final result!
0670/PLAYLCASTRATI

670 CASTRATO,
BBC Documentary

680 Fun Facts
about Castrati

Castration operations were often performed by actual butchers and only a tiny percentage of the boys who underwent the 'operation' ever actually made it onto the stage. The following link contains some more "Fun Facts" about *castrati:* 0680/CASTRATI

In case you missed it in the documentary, the following link contains the only known recording of a castrato. *Alessandro Moreschi* was in his mid-forties when he recorded Gounod's 'Ave Maria' in 1904. There has been a lot of debate about this recording. For most people, it grates on the ear. Was Moreschi just a bad singer? Some say he was mediocre, some say he was excellent but sang in a style that was tasteful at the time but not any longer. Some have suggested that the recording technology at the time was simply unable to capture the complete voice, which cut out nuance and overtones, and therefore, the recording remains just an outline of what the voice must have sounded like. It's also important to add that Moreschi was by no means a 'superstar' castrato like *Farinelli,* and this was well after the 'golden age' of castrati was already long gone. What are your own impressions?

690 Ave Maria
(Castrati)

0690/SINGER

20 Can Anybody Hear Me? Why opera sounds so different than other styles of singing

'Classical singing' or 'operatic singing' evolved before the era of electronic amplification. In order to be heard over an orchestra, singers needed to maximize their ability to be heard. Earlier we looked at various aspects of vocal production and saw that although opera singers sometimes do produce a lot of volume, they have also trained to maximize and exploit, to the fullest degree, the resonant qualities of the human voice. In the pre-microphone era, there were concurrently 'popular singers' who did not develop operatic technique, but were

then less likely to reach large audiences.
American inventor *Thomas Edison* was awarded the first patent for the microphone (*mic*) in 1877, although it had also been independently developed by Englishman *David Edward Hughs* and German-American *Emile Berliner*. And so, the game changed. Suddenly, it was no longer necessary for singers to, for example, develop *Singer's formant* or ensure that all potential overtones were freely ringing. Singers could have a much more intimate, 'speech-like' vocalism and yet still be heard over an orchestra or band without any problem whatsoever.
It may be interesting to note that when an opera singer sings directly into a microphone, the result can be rather ugly if the mic is primitive or not correctly positioned. Sometimes a microphone cannot capture the 'whole' of the voice, including overtones. The classical voice is meant to reverberate and be heard in a larger space to be correctly perceived and appreciated at its most beautiful, and can therefore be a challenge to mic and/or record well.

Vocal pedagogues generally refer to 1) classical or operatic singing and 2) non-classical or **CCM**, which stands for ***Contemporary Commercial Music*** singing which encompasses the following styles: musical theater, jazz, rock, pop, gospel, R&B/soul, country, folk, hip hop, rap, and alternative styles. One could say the CCM styles arose out of the sound of the speaking voice.

Classical singers strive for a *chiaroscuro* sound, which is achieved, generally speaking, when the larynx is low, the pharyngeal space is wide and the soft palate is raised to access bright head resonances. (To feel your own *soft palate,* trace along the upper part of your mouth with your tongue, from the base of your teeth backwards. At first, you'll feel a hard, skeletal structure which is the *hard palate* and soon the bone stops but the fleshy part continues – this is the *soft palate.* It is moveable and affects a singer's resonance and therefore quality of sound.) They also strive for smooth negotiation of the various registers of the voice (discussed below). Of course, as in every style of singing, the singer must also manage their breath and the co-ordination of all these elements as they dynamically interact.

In CCM styles the larynx tends to be higher and the pharynx narrower – in very general terms, it is a different usage of resonance. Also, vocal-fold closure and breath management can be different, as well as how the *registers* of the voice are perceived and handled by the singer. Again, singing is a complex and dynamic interplay of elements! Sometimes *belting* is a very desirable sound for some CCM styles. Since belting can be dangerous to the voice, CCM singers can undergo extensive training to 'mix' their *head voice* and their *chest voice* in order to achieve this exciting quality of sound, while maintaining vocal control and without injuring themselves. Some CCM singers are really masters of their instruments.

Click on the following Wiki-links for definitions of the terms

Belting: 0700/TEXT
Vocal registers: 0710/TEXT ,
Head voice: 0720/TEXT,

Chest voice: 0730/TEXT

730 Chest Voice

Here is internationally acclaimed singer and actress ***Audra McDonald*** who is not only able to sing in the music theater genre, but opera as well. Notice that the sound quality she chooses in this song is not really an operatic one. She is able to produce a *mixed belt* with great skill.

740 Audra McDonald Mixed Belt

0740/SINGER

Here is singing teacher Karyn O'Connor explaining a little about the differences in 'open throat' singing in classical vs. CCM styles. Following that, you can click on voice teacher Jeanette Lovetri's blog, as she shares her insight and opinions on classical vs. CCM styles of singing. It's entitled, 'CCM and Classical Are Not the Same'.

750 SINGING WITH AN 'OPEN' THROAT

760 Contemporary Commercial (CCM) and Classical

0750/PRESENT **** 0760/TEXT

Some CCM styles seek to smooth out, blend or 'mix' the registers of the voice, specifically the *chest voice* and *head voice* (for definitions, see above). We heard Audra McDonald doing this. However, some styles of singing take a different approach and actually accentuate and exploit register 'imbalances' - the greatest example being *yodeling* which we looked at earlier - but there are more subtle examples of this.

Here is ***Joni Mitchell*** in her early days, singing 'California'. Can you hear her flip-flop between a lower, meaty sound, and a very light, airy sound in her upper range? 0770/SINGER

770 Joni Mitchell

21 The Wonderful World of CCM

The intimacy and 'speech-like' nature of CCM singing opens up a whole spectrum of exciting sounds. Certain CCM singers are more consciously 'skilled' than others, but the personal, artistic and stylistic expression, and the recognizable individual qualities of a voice often get a chance to shine.

780 Louis Armstrong

Here is ***Louis Armstrong*** singing 'What a Wonderful World'. 0780/SINGER

Some people dislike the 'growly' quality in Louis Armstrong's singing, but many people simply love it.
To understand what is happening physically in this sort of sound production, we need to get to know the vocal anatomy even better.
Above both sides of the glottis are the *vestibular folds* also known as the *false vocal folds.* These are membranes that are also referred to as the 'superior vocal cords' ('superior' due to their positioning, not their quality!). They cannot, in fact, produce sound in the way vocal-folds normally do, but if they are adducted (brought together) and air passes through, they

produce kind of a growly, 'grunty' type of sound. This is a type of voice production that can be injurious, but the artists who use it can sometimes create a certain kind of earthy magic.

790 False Vocal Folds

In this short clip you can see the *false vocal folds* coming together, at times, actually covering over the vocal-folds.
0790/DEMO

800 Jersey Girl - Tom Waits

Here's the wonderful ***Tom Waits*** bringing his unique and powerful sound to us – growls, 'scratchy voice', belting, a heart-wrenching strain in the sound – and who would want it any other way!
0800/SINGER

22 No End to CCM

Just as it is beyond the scope of this little book to give a comprehensive account of the greatest opera singers past and present, it is also beyond its scope to survey the legendary music theater, jazz, rock, pop, gospel, R&B/soul, country, folk, hip hop, rap, and alternative singers. This book was meant to touch on aspects of voice production, shed some light on the matter, and examine a few different styles of singing that serve in revealing more about the human instrument.

Remember that for every subject briefly touched upon, there exists the possibility to go much deeper. For every subject, some specialist, singer, musicologist or other professional has devoted their life to its in-depth study. Let yourself be curious. Has this book answered some questions but raised new ones for you? Good. Go find out the answers.

Thank you for taking this 'journey of the voice' with me. I leave you with the equivalent of what is a vocal fireworks display. Enjoy! Here is Beat-Boxer Tom Thum –
'The Orchestra in My Mouth':

0810/BEATB

Technical and Legal Information

Reference numbers in the text contain *links* to documents and other content on the Internet. If you *click* on the left mouse button, the link will open up on your screen until you close it. Videos either start themselves of you have to do it manually with a *click*. You can stop and start videos using the *player menu*. Sometimes, you have to set videos to the desired starting point before watching them. If a video doesn't automatically start in full-screen mode, select this option from the player menu.
Interruptions are caused by low transmission rates on the Internet. Videos on the Internet usually come with advertising. This is common practice around the world, but it does ensure free access to valuable contributions.
The author has written this book with the utmost care. He checks the availability of linked content periodically and, if necessary, inserts alternative content. However, he accepts no liability for the availability of content introduced via "external links" to third-party websites. The respective operators are responsible for these Internet sites. When linking the external links for the first time, the author checked the third-party content for availability as well as any obvious violations of the law. At this time, the content was available

and no obvious violations of the law were evident. The author has no influence on the current or future design of the links, or on the content of the linked sites.
By integrating external references or links, the author is in no way appropriating the content of those references or links. Use of links is at the user's own risk. The author does not accept liability for any damage arising from users accessing external links. This applies particularly to malware such as computer viruses that may infect users' reading devices when accessing external links.
The author cannot be expected to undertake constant monitoring of the external links without any indication of availability, technical harmfulness or violations of the law.
As there is no intention of copy right´s infringements neither by the publisher nor by the authors we kindly request written notice (info@multi-media-books.com) in case a rights holder deems any link as an infringement. We will react immediately by eliminating the respective link. Neither the authors nor the publisher will accept any billings for cease-and-desist warnings in such a case. We kindly ask for generous support of our concept of introducing/publishing URLs of publicly accessible internet objects in order to spread valuable information about and to demonstrate examples of cultural heritages of Humanity.

All content published in this work is subject to German and international copyright and neighbouring right laws. Any use that is prohibited by these laws requires the prior written permission of the author or the respective right holder. The content and rights of third parties are identified as such. The unauthorised duplication or forwarding of content or complete sides is not permitted.